A Cure for Woodness

Other books by the author:

Continual Song
A Whole Bauble
The Music Laid Her Songs in Language
A Sinner Saved by Grace
Mid Life
The Quiet Works

A Cure for Woodness

(The Third Volume of *Music*)

☙

Michael Haslam

Arc
PUBLICATIONS
2010

Published by Arc Publications
Nanholme Mill, Shaw Wood Road
Todmorden OL14 6DA, UK

Copyright © Michael Haslam 2010
Design by Tony Ward
Printed in Great Britain by
MPG Book Group, Bodmin and King's Lynn

978 1904614 84 5 (pbk)
978 1906570 36 1 (hbk)

The author is grateful to the editors
of the following publications in which some
of these poems first appeared:
PNR, *fragmente, Skald, Angel Exhaust, Mid Life.*

Cover painting by Michael Haslam

Supported by
ARTS COUNCIL
ENGLAND

Editor for UK / Ireland: John W. Clarke

CONTENTS

INTRODUCTION

WOODNESSE

Wood is a dead word for Mad, well-rotten, nigh forgotten.

There's a handful of tricks, puns, quibbles, word-plays, rhymes, that have been basic to much English poetic practice. I suppose each generation, in freshness and excitement, discovers the same old puns and plays: woods and words, for instance. I'm just wandering the under-storey brush. Wood as mad, though, isn't fit for use. It was in decay in Shakespeare's day. Spenser uses it several times, but he liked to be deliberately archaic, and Shakespeare is possibly paying homage to Spenser in the line from *Venus and Adonis*:

> Life-poisoning pestilence, and frenzies wood

Earlier in the poem, I think he's making a joke, if only to amuse himself, describing the mutual lusts of the palfrey and the jennet:

> As they were mad, into the wood they hie them

I'm neither a proper scholar and philologer, nor a knowledgeable naturalist. I haven't taught literature or undertaken systematic research. I'll wander idly among old woods or poetries, sometimes not noticing what's under my feet, until something, some flower or bird, or word, springs to my attention, and, as it were, cries to be used.

Wandering the ancient wordlands (a nicely awkward mawkish phrase) I'm interested in such things as the meetings of obsolete, archaic, poetical, and dialect usages. An obvious example is the use of the second person singular: the *thee's*, *thou's*, and *thy's*. These were very common in my youth. They've been in decline, but are still common enough to pass unnoticed in the pub. They take the verb differently though: Thou knows, thou rarely knowest. Another example might be the construction *for to*, as in Shakespeare (*Venus and Adonis* again):

> Some twine about her legs to make her stay
> And all did covet her for to embrace

This construction is still common in Lancashire, but invariably contracts to *for t'*, which spoils Shakespeare's scansion. I air it in *Old Hall down in the Hollow*.

Other pleasures of idling include finding examples where there's been a bend, or cleavage of meaning. How was it, I might puzzle, that *buxom* shifted from 'pliant, submissive' to 'full-breasted'? O buxom lass! *Lass*, meanwhile, is fit as ever. And another case is *birdes*, which, I find, an editor has glossed as 'ladies; a high-flown term'. By the mid twentieth century this had become common, vulgar, lower-class slang, and thus offensive to the feminists, though 'ladies' didn't fare much better. It's the middle-class language police. But there is a problem with birds: it's mostly the cocks that sing. And there is sexism: why do we call chaffinches 'pinks', and not 'greens'? There's a pair below my window, chelping now. How gingerly the pink does tread the green!

I think it was Spenser who first led me astray with this word *wood*. Each stanza of *The Faerie Queene* is a delight to linger on, but there is no propulsion, and I'd be heedless of the plot if it weren't for scholars telling me what's what. And the bit of Spenser I like best is of the lightest: it's the contest between Perigot and Willye, from August in *The Shepheardes Calendar*. Here is Perigot describing the appearance of the bonilasse, the bouncing Bellibone (doubtless buxom in one sense, but not, alas, in the other):

> Per.   My sheepe did leave theyr wonted foode,
> Wil.   hey ho seely sheepe,
> Per.   And gazd on her as they were wood,
> Wil.   woode as he that did them keepe

This, possibly, set me off on the wrong track. I accepted the gloss at the back of the book: *wood*, mad, furious. Clearly there was little fury in the dumbfounded sheep: this was mad as daft, soft as a brush, wooden-headed, as thick as two short planks. Wood must be a wide word, wide as 'mad' itself. I put it to one side.

I was idly reading Chaucer – not the sort of thing I'm forced to... My first attempt at this Introduction was in doggerel. This proved self-defeating. Part of my tale is of crisis: of an attempt, and failure, to break with blatant rhyme and rhythm. I'm not forced, because my literary life is one of idle, amateur fun. I'd defend that against the professionals, if I had to.

It's good to revisit Chaucer – there's always something new to find. On a recent foray it was *Woodnesse* sprung up at me. There are many instances of wood and woodness in the corpus, but the most famous and the most vivid is probably the picture in The Temple of Mars, from *The Knightes Tale*:

> Yet saugh I woodnesse laughing in his rage

Here is rage, but with laughter, and that sense of stupidity I'd picked up from Spenser. I'm sure his eyes are brimming, bleared with tears. From here the word entered my ongoing scribble to emerge as a candidate for the title of this book. Then I thought

I'd better check my sense of the word, among the chance collection of texts on my shelves. And, at once, I suffered a setback, There's something mad about the ups and downs that versifying can involve.

For there was no doubt that the prime and dominant meaning of woodness was fury, anger, rage, and that was not quite what I'd had in mind. Typical might be Spenser's line (*F. Q.*):

That with fell woodness he effierced was

which could be translated as 'with fierce fierceness he was made fierce', unless perhaps woodness has some wider sense. That 'fell woodness' puts me in mind of Borrowdale in Cumberland, and is an impertinent example of what I. A. Richards called a 'mnemonic irrelevance'.

But I persevered. It was like when you set to rive out such weeds as nettles in the spring. Once you look for them, they're everywhere. The poetic record, between Chaucer and Shakespeare, turns out to be rife with wood and woodness: in all the main makars, in ballads, in Miracle Plays. Most affirmed the primacy of anger and rage, but I found enough with such senses as sad desperation, stupidity, eccentricity, and crazy sexual elation, to save my adopted word. Wood shared the same scope of meanings as mad: perhaps too close – maybe wood died in the failure to find a separate verbal ecology. And the word 'mad' itself is under attack: the medical profession don't use it; the socially-sensitive eschew it. If mad were to be killed, maybe we'd see fresh shoots from the trunk of wood. We need a common word for all sorts of mental nonsense.

Whilst doing this armchair and fireside research, there was a tale at the back of my mind. The bare bones are these. In one of the Three Futile Battles of The Island of Britain, brought about because of a lark's nest, Myrddyn Wyllt fought for Gwendoleu, possibly against Ryderch Hael (the Saesneg weren't involved). Myrddyn was so shocked by the fight that he fled to the forest of Celyddon, where he passed a length of time. I'm sure he fled in an absolute rage, but I suppose Geoffrey of Monmouth, in his typically fanciful garble, the *Vita Merlini*, is right that, though unfit for a return to the tensions of high politics, Merlin came to enjoy the delights of Nature, at least in summer-time. When this real madman emerges from the woods, it is as the perfectly legendary Arthurian magician, Merlin. I suppose the message I'm trying to formulate is: the woods are the cure for woodness.

And while I was drafting these paragraphs, in a Pennine garden delph, a few yards away from me a sparrowhawk just dived through the rhododendron and snatched the mistle-thrush, on one of her flights from the nest, in a sudden kerfuffle. And before I've revised them, the magpies have had her eggs. It's marvellous how consoling the cruelties of Nature can be.

In the compact country of England, there are limits to woodness. We go into, and come out of, woods. What else did I find? I liked the Gawayn-poet's metaphors of angry water in *Patience*:

> That the wawes full wood waltered so hye

and

> And ever wrother the water and wodder the stremes

Wood and water. What could be more therapeutic?

And there's a nice accidental pun arises around *Sir Gawayn* itself, concerning the 'wodwos' (that woned in the knarres) that Ted Hughes later brought to prominence. There are two schools of scholars here: some see them as satyrs, some sort of forest trolls; for others they're wild mad men, displaced human beings. The scene is set in the dark cold back-end of the year, fell winter-time. I think I can see them, in either sense, wodwos in Maytime, lolling in the bluebells by the stream, happily harking to the obsessive repetitions of the pinks.

ABSCENCE. DESPONDENCY. ODDNESS AND REGRESSIONS

'Abscence' is John Clare's habitual spelling (in his innoscence) of 'abscence', as in

> Abscence in love is worse than any fate
> Summer is winters desert and the spring
> Is like a ruined city desolate.

'Despondency' I lift from Wordsworth. Some of his more memorable lines are not his best, ('Resolution and Independence'):

> We Poets in our youth begin in gladness;
> But thereof come in the end despondency and madness.

'Regressions' were an attempt to retrace steps, to find another way out of the despondent absences of a seeming pointless plotlessness. This fails, but then I remember another way out, that seems to help.

The 'Oddness' is merely the oddness, to me, of having lived my life and pursued some sort of career, in poetry. Is there a cure for the woodness of it?

There was a time when I was strongly drawn to the lure of an idea of Absence. How can Emptiness shine like a tin can? The siren idea I drew from a concept formed from what I might call post-Symbolist French poetry. I remember hearing and reading such stuff in the 1970s. So much whiteness, nothingness, void, and silence, absolute silence. There was something almost mystical in the absence of God: you could almost worship the blankness. Out of this, I'd thought, could be made an abstract plotless sparkling pattern, sheer and clear of my personal feelings, now you see it, now you don't, in its significant insignificance, highly modernist, and, plausibly, impressive. In time, the shine went off this idea, but for a while it held me, and maybe left a legacy.

This French idea seemed to connect both with the Arcadian world of traditional French poetic diction, and with an emerging theoretical dogma that there is no passage between language and reality. But when I tried to wear this idea, to take it to heart as it were, I felt a phobia, a stiflement, a fear, a panic and a need to escape, to break out into real air. It were better for me to prefer a more English sort of poetry and thought. Language is part of Nature: a field of multiple animal choices, made by living wits and animal spirits. The mizzy bents and flaight are truly wet, and so's the sike-riddled shroggs I've seen me squelching up.

If this is the case then, arguably, Clare's abscence is less pure than the French absence: it is not so splendid a vacuity; it would be full of mud and cattle. His is regularly linked with his 'Mary', who was doubly absent as not with him, and, anyway, a delusion. But the mad delusion is real, a real *prescence*, one might say, in a real world:

The shaded lanes dirty
The ruts dribble on
And the sludges splash spirty
Where waggons have gone.

My own sense of absence has lately been a sight less mad, a puddle of lack, a mere despondency I called The Bus Pass Blues: I could catch buses to, say, Liversedge or Birkenshaw, and beyond, for free, but don't see why I should. I scribble on, but sense no living plot evolving: I just get older, and carry on. No lust drives me to seek the company of ladies. It's neither fully comical, nor deeply sad. There are slight amusements and small surprises. A roe deer just appeared in the garden delph. It was misremembering Wordsworth's 'madness' as 'sadness' that set me off on the woodness trail. Sadness could be simply weight. It's perhaps not too much of a Muldoonery to suppose that the tarn that the leech-gatherer stirs with his stick is the pond in despondency – the same as waters Bunyan's slough. Why can't I look for the steps?

It's been raining a lot this past year.

The poems themselves, up to, say, 'Wastes of The Picturesque' seemed to point to this mire of quag. One way to take steps appeared: to go back, regress to before the onset of doggerel, the blatant rhythms, blatant rhymes; find some purer, more old-modernist abstraction: a spread of poetry with no direction, breaking with the narrative impulse.

There is a field, a wood, a forestful of words, and one can scribble among them, even say things with them. They can be arranged, to export some obscure importance. My glad youth discovered what he called 'a languescope', which was only the wood of words. The field was there without him; it might divulge something about The Mind, but it manifested in Poetry. So in a sense Poetry could be competing with Psychology, Anthropology, Philosophy. The problem was that the sensed insights felt within this field could not be translated out into the surrounding fields of prose without loss of gist, without too much compromise. But perhaps if the languescope could be exquisitely arranged, its shining truth would appear self-evident. I thought an experimental modernism might be the way to go about this, breaking with syntax, narrative, traditional metre and paraphrasable content. Whether the results divulged merely my own so-called 'Unconscious' or the truth of the world would be for the world to judge.

I can still see my picture of languescope, but I failed, I betrayed my ambition. The work involved constant rewriting, in the course of which rhymes found lodging, metre was re-installing itself, and odd stories began to emerge.

One step back, and the word-world just looks mad. I lacked the confidence to over-ride self-doubts concerning charlatanry. I was too fond of the syntactic music of sentences to fulfil my intention. So I abandoned the grand abstract vision, and went instead for plot: pages, sentences, books, that had beginning, middles, ends, hoping only that something of the glitter and the glory of the languescope might cling to the tales. But this is only what our traditional poetry has always done.

The discovery of plots was not a matter of creative fictional invention, nor (after some experiments) the cribbing of existent story, but drawn from waves and cycles of personal emotional happenstance: patterns of illusion and disillusion, love and its loss, lust and its satisfaction, depression and elation, unconfidence and confidence, tragedy and comedy: personal, but common enough.

The absence, loss, felt in the pond of despondency, this last year or two, was merely the absence of event that might lift me off and give me plot. It was not too deep a pit: too shallow for grandiose self-pity. It was just that the writing was stuck – my daily life had become enviably relaxed.

In the past there'd been a sense of progress which led me to continually reject works of the past, as so many embarrassments. Now I'm possibly beyond embarrassment. I'd always had intentions about what I was making, but in practice, the practice was practice-led. Sometimes tricks of sleight would be required to align the work with the declared intent. I hadn't meant to go so deep into doggerel, but the scribble seemed to have its own intentions. Should I try to defend it, or make a break? Could I get back to less rhyme, less insistent rhythm; back to abstract plotless scope?

To kick-start the latter I threw in an old, neglected work, 'all blue chickens' (1972), which had been part of the languescope project, rejected for its apparent plotlessness. In a different kind of regression, I punctuated it traditionally, and brought it up to date by adopting more conservative notions of lineation. Then where? 'Heretical Expectorate' is a deep rewriting job. But here, it became clear, my scribble was not prepared to abandon its acquired habits. This ploy had failed. Some other tack was needed.

What I'd been lacking was spirit. Then a chance reminder, on Valentines Day, 2008, led me to throw in 'The Appendix: It' (1997), and think to reprint, here, again, 'A Lubrick Loosed', about it (two-thirds of wit and the tail-end of spirit. Why it is 'for Robert Sheppard' I might explain elsewhere). It might be re-invoked. It might re-crudesce and re-effulge: let it slip its lips, let it spit its pits, let it sprint in print. There might be something in it. Maybe it is the cure for woodness.

CURES

Did it work? I can't claim that the book ends in transcendent glory. Part of it is subdued, and if the pages cheer up a bit, this is partly age's venerable balm of Acceptance. It's the end of April now, and spring does its usual things. I've not lost the cycles of the year.

We know the standard cures for woodness, and I don't need to elaborate on them. Some cures are worse than the disease, and may exacerbate the madness. And, to be gloomy, Death is the final Cure for Woodness.

What have we? Here's a few. There's various forms of psy-chotherapy; drugs, legal and illegal; drink; religion; fresh love; poetry (reading and / or writing); and the Nature Cure, as The Butcher explained:

> In one moment I've seen what has hitherto been
> Enveloped in absolute mystery,
> And without extra charge I will give you at large
> A Lesson in Natural History.

I've a problem with 'Nature': I can't conceive of ought that's, finally, not-Nature. The Internet, Birmingham, The Home Office, The Neocons: none of these are unnatural. But, yes, the birds and mammals, streams and flowers and trees, the web of all living life and the pleroma of physical forces, with human-ity de-centred. There's a cure.

It was my intention that this book should be the third and final volume of a sequence called *Music*. I didn't know how it'd turn out, but this is it. *The Music Laid Her Songs In Language; A Sinner Saved By Grace; A Cure for Woodness*. The sequence begins with a sense of failure lifted by a willow-warbler. That deer in the delph last Friday lifted me again. I've sometimes read the claim that to find solace in 'Nature' is merely a (Wordsworthian) Romantic affectation. That's bollocks. It's clearly Universal. There are probably good evolutionary reasons for our being enlivened by the beauty of our sustaining ecology. But the hermits of the wood, or the monks on Skellig Michael had religious cause. God and his avatar, Jesus Christ – are they any use? – Well, not for me, not personally, not in my experience, but I'd like to quit this Introduction with a couple of lines from *Pearl*, from which that pair can't be excluded:

I rede þe forsake þe worlde wode
And porchace þy perle maskelles.

Woodnesse, Abscence, Despondency and Oddness

A BUNCH OF TALES

I caught a minute of what might have been the story:
      a stray pack of clouds in dark advent,
December hounds out on a run,
      down high brown moor-side. Then it's gone.
I nearly lost that one.

A bunch of dreamers in their nightwear
in a van who do repairs bring parody
to the affair. Black Mare. Crying hoarse
on the edge in high volumes of air. A black maria.
I was on that case and come to write
it out in a report, and there is no-one here
but mist and smoke, the stubs of burned forest.
Shafts of Phoebus glide the dusky glade and light
      on ferns, and fairy moats. And here I find
the comic in, just twiddling returns. I ask:
      has something happened on the plane of silence?
We can hear them drilling vacances.
Who are they? Silverers. How long
      until it clears? They're working late tonight in case
the other mirror errs. Is there another?

When it clears I'm living hand to mouth in some
inconsequential retail trade, where I hear something
      clearing the throat, like a street
prepared for a scream, but I returned to sleep on
to the end and then turn over
something soft as alpine cones of sweet ice-cream.

The scream wasn't loud enough then
to scare a bleeding clown,
        preferring quiet things preferably
accomplished songs:

In quiet hills nigh lilac light.
Like milky bottle-brushes of the bistort dock.
And how the dandelion lost her clock.
And when the sorrel found no will to fight
a rain of peace fell from the stars so hard
I took to shelter like a rabbit
in one of the delfstone tenements, just another
        snout pointing out until it stops.
The shower shocked.

I have bunches of lyrics. Rolling sheafs in clover.
By lad law lay by me. A ballad of
        a bad bye-law. A tale of love
adulterated in the hollows. Clouds
        of solitude and solace. Some found unknowns
I can't call out. The neighbours have me told:
        now tone that blessed silence down
for it's not very funny. Even by a clown.
They come down on us like louts
        just shedding windows, falling out
about the product of a kettlespout
in a cacophony. Say nought and kiss the ground.
They could have done with us, ughh, softness
with that tympany. The polymorphous parts
of sorry sores and soothing phoney story sorts.

Softness shifts with all the morals
of a dream, absorbing blame
and swabbing torn fool songs, the
suppurations of complete erosis.
They'll come bouncing back from the bounds
of sickly bliss back home, before long,
before the worm returns.

And here again the story night had come down
stormy wet – Safe behind the falling glass
a pair of clowns play weatherpersons
in the nude, performing turns – With starry gaps
of high renown.

The worm in the storm you can rest assured's
entirely meteorological, devoid of eggs and sperm.
The cry might sound alarming. Clear enough.
It's nothing personal. It could be couched
and maybe decorate with birds
in a conformity with pressures
sleeping in a calm, without a wind, unborn.

I come out boating from a flood of panic,
boasting when it sunk, and I too drunk
had left wry wit to mind an empty
quiet pint. I dined, and dimmed
the landing light in time to catch a flicker
under thunder of the supernatural estate.
A case of crashing, quaking glass.
I wake and sleep and drink and write to this effect.

The brain ought to be used
by now to sorting notions into
        untrue, useless, useful, true,
fate, luck, or rocks or sucks.

But it stuck
in a hook
of natural electricity

and I can't bring it to book
for all its long prehistorical tale.

Wait. Send out at ear to look.

The plangence of sirens
        and the silent trees.
The still stalls to pack
before another brainwave breaks

the waiting tissue for a notion
taken like a sneeze.

I shook:
        no words
that wild and empty notion took
but what eternal static takes.

Re-fill that space with predatory sea
and mountain beasts and birds.
        Re-Pair The Snakes.

BELABOURING IN REVERIE

Reface the lintel with a lump and scutch
and wire brush. Align and realign a line
by reck of eye and rule of thumb. Pull faces
thinking phrases for the lyric graces, lilac cordial,
vanilla curlew and so on. And hammer on
      until the limb's gone numb.
Break off to smoke, and idly play
      with mental prices: say at six, a florin,
ten, then two a penny, or an halfpenny a thump.

      And if I take a leak I'm at a loss,
a slash, a pee, a piss; that's my own
      at the aperture, open flies
at the back of the shed,
      the industrial waste. How come
thy moleskins seem defaced
      with lap-adhesive paste?
For lyric grace to dance you want
real English Fairies in the Poetry of France.
      Or have you shit your pants?
The fancy footprints and a flash that knocks
the sparky back and the electric blanks.
The labour clocks and banks the wages, docks deductions.
      Art is for the ages. Hard at work
against vulgarity. They say it wanks
to wage thankless assault on taste, by means of
      glorious plebeian ructions.

Clock off I think. The lads go for a drink. Remember when
us old ones sent the packing-lad to fetch a can
       of fresh phlogiston from the shops? Who was it caught us
pissing in the sink? The raffish electrician laughed:
       he's been entranced in psychic ops. We jeered to watch
the fiction-academics cross the picturesque green backs.
And how we camped about in birken copse and literally
       stumbled on a corpse....
Time warps against the clock.
The craft is gone. The wages stink. Get back to work or wash.

The roofers roof, the rafters quake the waters chop,
a quarter plops, the drawers draw the bankers draught,
the rowers row the plummet drops off summit top,
the miners mine the mine held up by props,
the idle idle round the house thinking to rhyme
the ore raw bouse. The butchers dress
       the tripe with cress. A plumber comes
to stop the pipe while cleaners wipe the mess.
       The village lads
and lasses lay about themselves with mops
in states of ripe undress. Each labourer may love
his or her next or nearest neighbour.
       Dreaming nakedness, I readdress thy face
my dear, in reverie wherever
there are dozens of us delving in the mass
       of gross behaviour.

FACE READDRESSED

When I was in, don't laugh at this, my own unknown,
a zero zone, I stumbled on a sylvan noumenon,
the nymph of sibling presence, her no less
            in all her polysemousness: her visage
in a cliff-face, riddled with erosion was
the face of beauty facing my semantic waste.

Her dress was greenest saxifrage, her tears were those of
            saturated ground; her intimate was toadflax,
ivy-leaved, in the crannied nook; her instep sprung
            dicotyledons; her familiars,
the balsam of far Himalayas, and her breast
or bust was rounded as the best image
            of blessed promise. In a fluke of light
her whole appearance aged and changed. The sound
            of water which the wind had drowned
came round again deranged.

The hills above, beyond, around
            this lovely clough
and scene of folly, barely stood
            a blow so loud;
lay bruised but proud,
            treeless and melancholy,
settled into senseless prose,
            devoid of polysemy.

RUNNING TO METER

Winter came after us, running the moor edge,
numb sky curling over bogey holes,
        and I don't mean golf but *gulph*,
as beaten down beneath a welkin dull
our two young lover souls, out courting on a ledge,
look small down in a dell, and I don't mean computer,
rather something covert, steeped in stealth –

But, truth to tell, it
now was many years ago
we fell down to the hall
and the derelict mill with its weed-full yard
        and stagnant well, and spent wealth.

I never. Did we? Was it we made love
or love we made, by the wall in the snow,
with classic echoes off a distant sledge?

Had we not done it up against the stone wall-edge
of rockery with snow-in-summer, decorating blocks
of, it was not your ideal gardening rock-garden, no but
somewhat sunken, street stone-setts
and millstone blocks on topsoil. No hard core foundation.
Ever.
        I know well the poignancy of courtesy,
if as and when, my Mother said, you take her out,
be nice to her. I gave my pledge.

We'd had nothing to eat and the mine-mouth hole
hung between foreclosed and wide a-gate,
and there we ate meat sandwiches, I had badly prepared,
and could barely pronounce myself the gurgling
nearer sound inside a drum. Wet lugs. And as a pair
we looked upon the plain down south-south-either,
somewhere in high moorland, anywhere. Sat up
      on Rivington Pike if you like. Beset, if it's the summer,
by the bugs. Aye bumble bees. There'll be a Reservoir
for sure we understood as public good.

Note how old worths and the accorded settlements adhere.
How plangent and how bottomless a bucket goes for scrap!
      I paused, running to meet her, check the stock
and cross one off. Head on.
      Just where I lost the van somewhere a
wan-ness won. And when I thought I didn't love her then
      it happened that I heard the siren
for the flood up valley wood.

LYRIC IN BLEMISH

For these blemishes in the poet's style are of such quantity and magnitude as to deny him even a hearing from those who love a continuous literary decorum and are grown intolerant of its absence.

ROBERT BRIDGES on GERARD MANLEY HOPKINS

Blemish is the native tongue
    I speak in song
        in quiet hills' nigh lilac light
        small traffic and less speech
and write ways wrongly wrought, unblessing
and unteaching what I meant to preach
unblushing and unleashing
    such a blow as issues
in a ruddy bluish bruise
    and blear verbal abuses
that may stick as tissues to a bursted peach
to blot the rot and pipe distresses,
kisses, liquefaction, tears and tresses
mess the hair: a blasted blamed contusion
    and a vulgar madder bloody cheek
to titter dissonantly melodic confusion,
blemish curses ripen ripe
    pipsqueak to fruiting screech
round which the *quiet hills* fall into *damson night*
that boasts *less traffic*. Then the lyric wishes
an unblemished peace
    and quietness to all and each.

OLD HALL DOWN IN THE HOLLOW;
SPRING UP SUNNY BANK

The hall stood empty in the hollow now for years.
Elated yearly, swallows haunt the empty court.
At dusk a woman in her nightwear disappears.
The purlins rot, the rafters drop a weight of slate.
Creepers assume the mistal stalls.
Wind and frost'll finish off the walls.
A colony of rodents holds the floor.
A bluff wind lifts the rook-flock off the trees.
The wind turns wet and colder.

It's fictional, vestigial, Symbolic Hall.
Only the spate-spill down the hill, eroding silicates
of coal and shale is real. The fabrication falls
through the decades without repair. Were April here
personified, there had been nothing here to hold her.

The old mock music hall of fools,
trash rubbish, dump of ghosts,
unsightly sprights, the prank-faced fakes,
with their out-dated passes franked:
Notice To Quit: Clear Out Old Hall Enclosure.

The elder elves'll not have time to
elevate themselves
with umbelliferous umbrellas.
One boggart semi-derelict, unsold, ceramic
with a chip upon its shoulder.

A bill of sale. Vacant possession of a pile
devoid of denizens.
In single syllables:
the hall is to be sold as a (disanimated) shell.

Fruit drops over the roof; elder roots in footings;
grass and birk takes troughing; alder, clay-baked
broken drains. The trickle drops, the sylvan droops,
a crown of plumes, the living dead, the sullen
nettle groups, the open doorway to a leaning shed.
        The mossy gate-stoops.

        A line of ghouls along the wall in mist
ejaculate their last, and re-adjust themselves
as triste, as sadly-blissed and detumesced.
The rotten shame itself expressed disgust.
Another April reappears distressed
and runs uphill against the drains.
In wind, the rooks enjoy a tournament of argument.
The hail flew horizontal. So it blew
        through drops and stops.

There's something nibbling at the well again
in quiet. Waters gurgle, gutters scoff.
Rafters dip and stone-slate slips.
The porch is drawn with creepers round the mouth.
Time flies about the mouth of miry rough.
Old hall stood empty in the hollow now for years.
There was a lot of water in the rain today.
There is a sentiment instilled of long decay.

Umbral eaves and sallows court in ashen shade.
The little falls a quiet source of water noise.
There's something feeding there. It could be supernatural,
or something suppering on stagnating emotional
or other suffering. I let it out

down by the wicket gate with the evicted spooks
and settle as the purple drains
to dusky-coloured sorts of dot, fickle imaginings
of mimic things, free of dependants, stepping out
in fantastic apparel. Then I pack it in
a trunk of props.
      The price of fancy drops.

I came back to the bar to find it emptier
than it ever were before. I must address myself
the solitary auditor, my own report. I needn't shout.
      I cut down oak-wood steeps, round by
Old Hall and down the disused railway steps
to where the bus-stop is and out.
My thought and feeling set at nought.

I reckoned up the reach of emptiness.
There's just another glass.
A schooner stranded on the bar.
The bottle-bank. The ground in sound. The way
a wet wind pastes the patching placards,
filling wind-holes, nailed to the remains
of wooden frames.
      The endless rhyming drains.

With secret joy the plumbing lapwing wreaks its call.
The sike is feathery with spate. Each bird with a
cloaca maculates. Erosion riddles banks.
A mass of water acts as if its gravity
had purpose
          and no sooner you get up to date
than with the sediment bed down with clay and clam.

It's still called Sunny Bank in any weather.
I saw April shining naked in a shower,
peering through a pair of glasses from a shake-hole
on the heath, or I'd been scrambled on a ferrous
landslip, down the dip. Lights extinguished just as if
I had got strangled by the throat at dusk.
          It must have been some ghastly private tangle,
getting stuck in clay and clam,
          with ewe and ewer, avenue
and Anglican and yew, with tup and stopper,
ram and lamb and udder-dam, with shaggy wether,
shit and slit, with cleft and quick to get it up
and mix with bluebells, ramsons, doe and buck.

There was a kid (of billy-nan)
who pushed his baby sister in a pram,
but when he came to the steep top
of Cinder Lane he let it go, to watch it run
and crash into the trees down at the brook.
And though the babe came through unscathed,
and Wickedness was saved by Luck,
he hardly ever pushed a pram again.

Give us a break, ye scholars schooling us
syllabic feet, caesural intervals, some solemn
syllabus without the holy silliness. We should be
taking syllabubs off buffet trestles, making accolades
of ale for Easter Day, or plucking milkmaids
from the ditch, or counting daylight starrinesses
in a play, or turning tap to faucet for a
          sylvan facet, greeting urinal ceramics,
piddling with a fiddle at a gala, calling
          pluvia, a pluvial, a pluviala:
on a day like today. I could be tumbling with April
in the pleromatic washer waste, flooding in erosion,
sensing erotic emotion, laiking at collage
with lap-adhesive paste, or slapping brushes
          from a bucket of slaked lime.

You have over-egged the pudding up the English rough.
Juggling and giggling and jiggling and gurgling mean
          next to nothing. Readers have read enough.
Please try to write more seriously stiff and thoughtful stuff.
You only bluff your edging precipice with guff.
You overplay the clown. Infantile fancy makes you mime
the peewits' tune. The real green plovers piping
up and down the bank's field ground complain.
          Real poetry is tough.
Yours is a frothing at the mouth in rhyme.

Abashed, ashamed, I saw myself into the court.
I thought I saw myself in two. There stood the hall,
a core all hollow, falling dead in time.

Falling out is still in love. A stone's throw
from an empty can you feel the water as
the pebble plops. Plough sow and reap just as
they say, and someone steals the crop. You saw
your trunks off for to coppice. Young spring greens
your wooden top, but all the while the store
of silver mental cutlery I call Old Hall depletes
in dribs and drabs and drips and drops,
and by the time you fix the stop-tap all is lost.

      The time comes when the very spot is brightly ripe
for redevelopment. Whoever harbours the old spirit
gets the chop: turfed out by landscaping contractors
at considerable cost.

      Let old men drink. Just give us one last spirit
wing-twist, neck the bottle, top to cap,
ah *pluvial,* I do remember thee, as once
with nasal rank in ramsons, young leaves burgeoning
however poor a beauty, I played the young fool
with the masking-face of bluetit. Please absolve me
or ablute it. An idea of love. I bought it in
the innocence of puberty, when everything was
younger by an age. It was the innocence of lust.

Carrot and Kale among the vegetables spill out
from the Old Hall kitchen garden, seeding to spread
the meadow. Carrot grew but scrawny root yet
flowered wild. Sprout has leapt the stile and makes
escape into the hayfield. Vocables are called
but can't be fetched into the fold.

      A sedentary stone is truly mossed.

Sunny Bank come to sudden fullness: springs a warm
swift rain and greens that moss on stone to sheen a lane
with marigold and pink purslane.

April through June a sudden cold can pitch a watcher
as the shadow into ghost-time: one upon one's own,
who looks across to see the sad one hanging
under eaves in rope.
    And there's another one that feeds
down at the well now lopes off lonely,
thinking badly of the disinvestment of the soul.
It leaves in woodness with a thatch
for ought to nest in. One has grazed
his hands on golden sandstone out of love, and come
as almost reconciled to recognise the redevelopment
as what things will look best in: swish partitioning
of flats, wanting a word that's posher than apartments,
    fetching many grand.

The sun goes in and comes back out again around the clock.
Some days the sun shines but on other days it rains.
Now shining buggies line the wall.

But one last sudden sunless gape at the cloud-riven
steeps, and there's some noumenon appears redressed,
a fine sylvan phenomenon that's come to spark and die,
and leave one wordless while the wealth arrives
with newer human beings and the bogey-shade
retracts, retreats in spirit. One goes quietly now
    so as not to stir it.

The ghost is feeding at the well just now,
appears and reappears, regular as a stranger
to consciousness, caught up for a moment
in a trap-like trance, as possibly
        a dreamer at the bar,

a mirror-glance, a wry light smile.
It shall be sweetened, grazing docile,
while evading eyes of all the other
supernaturals, as those, it says,
        I helped betray:
they're bound to be evicted by the stile,
and be imprisoned in some set-aside
as fenced for wild, or laid and made
into a set of solid beech-wood benches, banks
for aged sentiment and pensive,
        pensioned reassurance.
Rest Awhile, now prop thy stick.
I think thy thirst appeals to drink.

And you can hear earth-movers work
in either dust or shaly mud beneath
the beech-wood scar. The Old Hall grounds
are being radically re-arranged,

but the evicted ghosts, I say sincerely, they
were mercifully mostly fanciful
        images of endurance, often merely
pagan-light, as April,
        ale or daffodil.

WASTES OF THE PICTURESQUE

1.

An art of ruins wastes and wrecks has left a late-
romantic artist vexed, perplexed before a space
of nothing but a tract of wretched text, a vacant complex
he suspects means nothing more as message or
as metaphor than merely private wreckage of his own
poetic sex. Well he might draw these wastes
of the picturesque; well might he sketch a pathos
in a few pathetic jokes: black porters on the froth
and stuff, drawn struggling up the sliding shingle
bearing barrels on their heads; chests on the water
or a schooner on the bar. And then and there
a cry ejaculates from stair-head steeps, and echoes
in trance deeps. Could be a figure on the landing
where the shadow creeps. And when the sun went down
it all became one vast black mass. The earth rolls back
and yet the sun still sets.
      It's not some actual desolate coast
but just a desk at which to write an uneventful
picaresque where nothing happens, and then nothing
happens next, beneath a leaden sky, a vague context,
the where in which the images exist: decrepit shed
of blackened brick corroded red, a scent of seepage
pungent from the jakes, a ketch that bumps the landing
      twice, and rolls back on the rocks. *Wet feet. Wet socks.*

2.

The full illumination came: a streak of lightning
as it forks and strikes, and silhouettes a tall ship
in distress, a splintered spar, the rigging rent, and yet
the sheets were paper, neither rope nor cloth.
The schooner on the bar stood empty, foam-ringed
from the beer. The artist scrumpled up the wasted sketch
and tried to make the same again, waste of the picturesque.
    The sun drinks oil off dreck and sets. The lightning
bolts the eyes to stark despair. A flock of bits and specks,
of gulls and rooks in silhouette; the gully wrack
the sea rejects, its plastics, polystyrenes, corks
and tattered nets. From stair-head steep
look down trance deeps and hope to sleep.
    Begin again then from the ending: wakes
and comes down from the landing, far inland. The damp
hearth of an underdwelling, back to earth, beneath
a dripping cliff. The brook sounds louder under overclouding.
Someone shouting out *Blue Murder!* Surely Emptiness
is no sort of Container. Better shut up shop.
The inner sphere has left a misty residue of atmosphere
bereft. The empty nest did not contain a
living soul. No sense of deeper meaning holds.
The waste lies cold. Self-pity demonstrated impropriety
    and isn't pretty but in poetry, *I sat me down.*

3.

I sat me down upon a block of frosted stone
to sense an inner vista, lyrical and piquant
as it melts and seeps. I weep tears pretty well.
The swell rolls forward within bands of rush,
recoil and hush. The bay curls slowly like a long-unbroken
song. The night falls black, the hulk falls dark, the dream drops
steeply down a rocky drop. A white foam takes the rocks.
I stumble back towards the bar to talk, but meet a hush,
a wake, recoil and rush.
            A drum rolls up against the landing.
I'll be drinking in the shadow lee of self-estrangement.
Water calms behind the quay. The fork and silhouette
can be confirmed, confined, forgotten. Crumpled cans
down on the sand contain an emptiness
whose drawing fills the picturesque.
            A tidewash wreaks an excremental flotsam
twisting up the shipping creek. A sick burlesque
here belches to a retch, at such a sentimental
sweet romantic mix as had maintained the picturesque.
A stinking tank of plastic bottles, stray swamped
scaffold planks: the landing shed is stacked with
broken pictures, sketches, the aborted wrecks, the subjects
in poor taste, mere pictures of the wrecks of waste:
black clouds and ripe sunsets. The lightning forks
            again and silhouette. *Clank chains and hoist containers.*

4.

Come something and save us
from the raucous talk and racist jokes,
the empty schooner stranded on the bar,
the desperation at some engine failure
and one's own mental defects, except
        I've seen some dreams with steeper drops than this.
Counting steps up to the bar.
The breakers ease the stiflement all night at heart.
        A vessel sinks in drink.
Take one last turn across the neck.
A septic yellow sky infects a last glimpse of the wreck.
The sun drinks oil off dreck. Guts get upfetched.

It's lovely though as after then to bathe the feet
in wet fresh frothy shingle, lathering and lounging in
the backwash with some fussy longing, watching
        heavenly-like glimmering across
the surface of the deep, and come to calm
and float asleep, to the repeats of the poetic
pebble-chafe effects, until
        the glass falls further in the dark and there lay
on a raft the total wreck, bereft
upon the waters in resumed distaste, the waste
a life collects, the written works,
        the picture wrecks.

Regressions

ALL BLUE CHICKENS GO TO GOODGOLD (1972)

Start City Star! A swarm through grass
towards a grasp of city came.
That had to come, I knew as soon
     as I stopped to light a match on stone.

The wandering child across the carpet, rich in image
comes towards the city, in a dewdrop, in a
     clod of earth,
and vessels in the light-lines hover over
children dropping out of binding hoops.

With Angel Blue!
     The sky has been tickled by feathers.
It's a bird-bright angel, fallen from the roof
onto the tongue.
     Gold pulls dreams into a compact.
There's a scope the words have not yet culled.
Frames of artifice out in the suburbs stretch
the city patch-work – a mosaic
     of varicoloured glass – within the net.
Small fry like stars slip through, and hook
     onto a feather.

The bridge devolves across the passage.
Cold wind out across the sea. Cold passage
out across the sand.
    The rain refreshes faces in the dark
and there's a memory of water
    and the passage here.
The boats bob on the sea.
The sea occasionally belches,
    and this worries me
more than the fact,
a cosmic brood of frightened dancers
    has hatched in a darkened room.
The scope includes slivers of paths
that may not be on the map.
A brand on water fizzles in the dark.
The room rushes to meet us, but it flows right past
leaving a minute brightness
    at the centre of a startled moment.
The heart of the city of glass collapses
in a release of blood; identity
    has re-become the stars.

Below the granite headland, underneath the stars
the faded yellow that the day has been
has found a door that's lit.
    But the stale tide crept as flat as a pancake.
But in an hour a light-house, but in an hour a light breeze
made the morning fritter crisp,
    and fog lifted a curtain on
the dark grass ring.

A path from birth to birth and thus
the meaning of the one landscape revealed
a silence on the growing heap of glowing gold,
a stolen treasure.
      All Good Children sail the Ships
all through the night, but we have passed across.

A Gold bounded by Blue. These two are intimate.
Light Blue for Infant Boys. An everlasting
      home in heaven.
Save Time and Space. Keep Quiet
crossing frontiers.
      Blue Boys! Silent Heavens! Blow Horns!
Sun blast the key of gold. An everlasting home
is no parental home. (Now feel your Pulse.)

Configure Realms! The figure in a moment faded.
Radiations from the hearth
      delight the strangled matter.
After the sun sank, water went
      where sewage goes. The sun-globe broken
on the wave prevents accumulation
      after dark.
When cloud-lights fail, it dances down
dark suffocated in the story-matrix.
      Comes Relief
and forms of men
      are changing money in an endless market.

I entered the creaky dream-house, death.
The waves beat on the shore. A dead sea-gull
lay on the shore. Blood, tar and pebble, there.

Waves feed on the quiet matter of thought.
I walked towards the house where weeds and grass
grow round the door.

Growing Reasons in the Quiet Town.
The chickens fed on bread of heaven.
Me, with the Empty House Greens.

A newspaper is blown along the beach.
A man was scattered to the stars.
A light-bulb sways in blue light.
The scope of tongue or dream.
A sun-prince in the house of grace.
Grace hidden in the leaves.

Walking to the edge of sleep,
it ended steeply.

The silent troops of no good
        are endlessly waiting for trains, but there's
a trap-door flaps open on ocean.
        He woke at the boundary. Everything
stretched away.
        The prints on sand are of children
coming home to change from haze
        to graceful evening light

after days of brilliant horror. When
        the dream ended, the figure
is dissolved into the mouth.
        The prints on sand are of
sun-light and imagination only.
        Against tides of image
        shut the door.

When time has gone slow in the market square
on a slow afternoon, the water bubbling there
as time runs out as good as gold
        from the silent retort, and the heap accumulates
outside my window, and everyone's gone dead or home:
        Then the chickens fed on bread of heaven, and again,
and it's so easy, slowly quiet in the silken, or the silent space,
        the sea knows only where the water
slowly goes.

In his own space he moves through his idiom of rooms:
Here I felt strange today.
        Clock Hands at The Market Fountain
sat on stone,
        then turned and Walked Through Town.

The blue infant is dancing in a silence
in an enclosed space, lit-up by mirrors.
Street-lights burst to bloom.

In the summer, burning suburbs blaze
        a purple-blue. The feathers flock
as blood, as water drops, as globs.
        The light through frosted glass
catches hot water so that glass reflects
a stream of water-angels
        celebrating the electrics.

A man who roots and values gold among his sorrows
stands in grey, failing-refreshing rain,
        among the choking weed,
upon a cliff of sand.

A drizzle blanking blanket is occluding out to sea
        as murder-purple wracks the squalid dream.
The sun-set glimmers die on fallow fields.
The rich land grows dark.
A flaming head has disappeared
and darkness spread like marmite.

Silent heaven blue in contact with the gold.
The empty house deep green in which the boy
was left alone.
　　　The blood-blown body. Pounding waters. Pounding feet.
Across dark water, breath and pace of oar.
Dark land-marks shift.
　　　Our home's the inn with lights.
　　　Our house is in the light.
Blue time with lanterns. Blue azure light.
　　　A network of powerful lines on the sea.
A boat-man between sky and land.
A shifter after drift-wood for a flesh-fire,
　　　smoking on the head-land.

The comets streak and shock the sky.
This is a map I write *The Dark* across
　　　the wave-breath and the song-flesh
sung far out to sea as hands can stretch
the fingers of the land.
　　　And I can clock and check the trade.
The clock ticks on. Accounts accumulate
　　　and settle in my reckoner.
The light a fallen man. I laugh like feathers
at the mockery of this.
　　　A burst of thunder.
　　　I walked home. Expelled,
I fell like feathers,
　　　fishing for stars.

Shouts of boys playing foot-ball
        on the cowboy-field.
Green shirts print
        the plague of dream
so early on.
There was a castle over-looked a beach.
        What emerged at dusk begins to scrape
its fingers. Then the changes begin to begin.
        The morning wind billows the sails.
Cloud-stacks are gale-high. Feathers float
out in the blue of the bay. A sail
        panics and flutters. Cloud-stacks are
gale-high. Feathers float out
        in the blue of the bay.
Turmoil on horizon gulps all helpers
in apparent calm.

The King Died. That was the dead sea-gull. All the
buses stopped. The Queen came slowly to The Throne
while we played foot-ball in the rain.

      In all the roar of traffic there was nothing like
the silence of the room.

      Thunder burst out of a greater silence.
I was flashing through blue rooms in pain,
and each blue room another flash of pain,
and then a green pram silence and a singing
      in the ears and a confusion as to size.
The fear I think was just the fear of plain
dull silver and the sight of scissors.

      Opening the tomb they found me drawing milk.
That's when the king died and the buses stopped
and some voice said that, No There Isn't
      Any Bridge At All.

A girl lay naked on the beach,
    as moist as venus. I was washing up
the tea-things, not to see
the sun corrupt the dream, the sun in so-doing
    burgle the room.

I'd carry slops on the receding tide. O Aphrodite! O
My Lady of The Slop! among the flowers,
grape-fruit, cabbage-leaves and urine. Oh,
    and at the ending of a long hot day,
the rubbish feeds the sea.
    At low-tide cloth, picked and dropped
by undulations slaps.
    The wave has come to meet me,
on the traeth. This is the stretch
I carried the can across the wide wet sands.
    A trade of carnage dashed against the walls
subsides, leaving time stretched emptily away.
    This is Standing on the Abrupt Hill. This is
Choking Shine. He fell like hell,
and metallurgic fluid set along the channelled sand,
with there a feather, floating down onto the blue
blue circle, oil, wax, dung and feather; here
the battle was, as thick as myth, the robes and stick
    float on the sleek and black
beneath a hollow morning moon,
    and after laughter, feathers of a mackerel-line
slick and go slack.
    Along the shore-line treasures face the muffle
that was after dark, after-dark, the afterdark.

Along the shoreline, feathers are the only trace.
   A fast stream enters in his lack
on fine ideas. The thought of slaughter grabs him
like a woman. Currents slide
      through sheen and slime. The consonants
reflect a brittleness between the vegetation
and the darkness, and the onward-flowing liquid
      of the water.
Droplets glisten in the grass, and juggernauts
roar down the arteries, and he must strip
      his clothes off, splash into the shock
of water as the shaft illuminates
      his face and dripping water.

Fresh water bubbles in between the slabs of stone,
and mosses in the glow are now invisible.
A head of light waves through the eyes.
The flowers are all spoiled with water-bubbles.
      In the clearing, woods are blue behind the light,
and light leads to the dark again.
The wet is naked and is vulnerable.
      Her still arms hold him as he gazes out at signs,
occluding possibilities with fingers,
      fusing outlines in retort: a clouded glass,
the worst is past.
      To outline grace, haze is included. There's
a chaos out which way I go. I find a prism
key to grace inclusions. The reflex of water
gives a ground of dissolution. In developments of city
      we are everywhere expressed.

She's the blue of atmosphere in spot-light spot-lit, or
        hot water poured from kettle-spout.
I closed the door and found myself locked in a clearing
where big men are hacking flesh to stripes,
or hanging out where angels fly, in moist
        and glittering air! The sun seems to
disperse the clouds. It's cold
but fairly blue out there.

An order stills the land. And adults stalk in silence.
All their brains were in the stars;
        While in a shining dome or sphere
an Empire closes at the dead end of a line
and gas-lights disappear.
        The fish flow through the air.

And birds sing in the wet:
        a growth of song in under-brush.
The small fish penetrate my net like stars!

To sail across the dark to meet her,
        fade in sunlight, agony, grey skies at noon;
the agony, of sunlight striking metal.

        Sea-gulls have set up a squall.
        The clock ticks slowly.
        Hollow. Ashy. Grey.

Wet *Saelige,* wet silage and wet Holy Days!
    "in days of rain
a sad wet haze hung in the happy valley,
up between laughter and tears, one hand
against a dripping tree, and through the trees
one city of the sun stands still,
    and graces haze the wooden glade."

It is a tangled glittering in the hazel twigs
that's lucid,
    " harp a graceful music
in the curve of bay
    before it turns into hysteria and aches."

The cow-bells ceased to tinker with the clouds.
The glass has fallen.

Grass has gone to glassy gold.
The blue one gone for good.

A Light!
What startled hurts?

HERETICAL EXPECTORATE

Elasticated static spans and snaps. How you do love
what you do fear. From sunblind spots
        behind the bluff, electrocuting angels open fire:
the squiggler in the gulch gets shot.
        It crackles and it spits:
a living coal in fire, a voodoo gob, a soul outlaw,
animate gist, a spirit of heretical expectorate
got spat. It sizzled on the hob. It frazzles
        like a hair on fire, expiring
as a thingum on a pyre: so white, so fair,
so wasted by their higher fire-power.

It speaks its last, that *I was in their sight.*
They held their finger on the trigger and they pressed it tight
and I was dazzled by the light. And so they shot
that verminous and spiky sprite. They caught it
in a flinch of pure fright, and now it's not,
and all the same the sun burns still
        bar cloud and night.

What remains of the thing that is not has got
        binned in a box. It is remembered for its
holly-leaf-like smacks and smashing glass effects,
and by the tales: how it spat back, how it took knocks
and how it turns to spring from trash among rejects.

Will it not come to life? It does look
somewhat mournful, greening on a stump of stone
like so much moss in some light sunny rainspot.
It gets cross, irated scornful of its death and suchlike loss.

My guess is yes, it either lets genetics take its habits
as it learns, or simply jumps to life in spite.
        It gets a horn full on the head and grows
from tininess a tool, a tail, from which it
gives a toss. And in the bliss of this it grows heretical,
        hallucinate, utterly unruly and quite bright.

A LUBRICK LOOSED

It's like a sly evasive wit. It's like a shy reflection on a set of cellar steps. It's like saliva on the lips. It's like a highlight to the eye; it's like a lubrick or a trick. It twists the tongue into itself as it escapes.

I should have loved to lure its source of likeness in, to organise the making of a threnody for when it's gone. I could have thrilled to sense it shiver as it takes the bait. But as it spilled its reputation surreptitiously it left a trace, a blank, a tip, a bit of luck. It gave the slip.

I read it once and swallowed my acceptance of the verdict and the sentence: to be taken down by hollow lingual alleys and be bound to serve a term of time in dispute and in disrespect, then to be smothered in expiry in the matrix muff of nothing minus happiness, and any skin thrown in the lake of dreary slime that's drying to a bed of crusted flakes.

A shadow in the shedding light that slowly showed descending stone, I sniffed the fungal passage must effect arising from the trap for soil and waste below the cellar steps. It must affect it to be dead. It should be buried. As obsequy, let it be said:

How lavish of its offices it offered silken thread, and yet how tacitly and well it kept the spell of secrecy alive within the cell, not letting any ghoul of imputation or the ghost of a suspicion ever touch or taint a hair – if it had any – of its silver head – but put a subtle finger to the lips, blinked as an imp, emitted squeaks, and with a crooked limb it shut its lid.

Cures for Woodness

STARLIGHT DATES THE PALM

Recycling a debacle, obsolete poetic phrases,
Imperial Glory, Arabian Nights, post-Keatsian
Moonshine moments, Oriental Monuments,
The Vintage Grapes of Ruby Wine,
        the cluttered furniture of rich
idealistic spaces, endless balm of rhymes with calm
but weary, I lay down in some
        Victorian Oasis, plush with gaudy
faded graces, dozing in the *crystal stupor*
I had patented my own, by chance I found
        as good as new, unused, unheeded,
and for less than half-a-crown, a line it feels
my life has needed, and I hold it now, cupped
in my hand, and trailed along my arm, the title
Supra:
        Starlight dates the palm.

Good stuff at that. I reckon I could pass it off in story
as a fruit-juice, or a jewel lost
        from old Fitzgerald's *Rubaiyát*
for, say, two guineas as reduced, 'at cost',
The Ruby Gate of Dawn, the poet's loss, I don't see
        who's abused, or where's the harm.

PRINCE PHOEBUS COLUMBUS

From the Globe of first albescence unto rubicundity
the glabrous column of the day arose
        or penetrates The Gates of Dawn.

The ruby gate is widened for the pomp of his estate
plunged plumb into the orifice of rubicund
to surface in the palace of the sun: to globe the rise
with presence as the pillar of Apollo,
        filling fuller: to the height of pure profundity
and pillowed in the cumulus,
        the glory morning convolulaceous
raising trains in twine, combining columbine
with honeysuckle and with eglantine, sweet briar
        rubus rubiginosa with convolvulus woodbine
and stretching Phoebus higher.

Red rim. Blood run to head
by rose osmosis, in the dreaming place of youth.
I do so fancy buxom earth in all her finery, complicit
        and compliant, bent into the light of orient:
Twin shadows pair, prepared to stand
        as stanchions for a stanza. They appear
to let dilate the ruby gates. Too late to stop
twin palms spring dates. The pit itself is labiate;
one kisses and the other spits
        warm rain at sunrise
with a west wind running east to the embrace,
a sudden pose, to gloze over indecency,
        what grows, to kiss what glows.

It was just so. The prince rode on his way
with his fluff-feathered phallus undeflated,
        so delighted with the chaffinches at play in daylight
with the breath and aura of the palace gated
        for his entry into space.

But there he felt a sudden drop.
        There was a sheet of gloom draped on his office.
Oddness turned between portcullis
        and the gated wall. It is his head
that's on the shilling, seeming sanguine,
it's him stamped upon the golden plate.
Stop faking fantasies once and for all:

        let soul and soth both droop with sloth
into the soup or broth, but stir and drink
the stupor with a lengthy ladle.
        Phoebus fears there's no way through
        from grave to cradle.

And where the prince rode, there it befell,
he fell and left the bridle. This could rhyme with
bridal well, and touch the brooch worn at the throat
with a stabbing lump and thought
        emotionally fraught:
there's been too much romance at court.
I should have bundled up the royalties as fiction,
written treatises upon poetic diction,
        but for Majesty
I've nought to show.

The sun was hot, the mating languorously slow,
    up to abatement of the sport
with many bored of dalliance, either with glamour or
    proprieties of grammar and the, if pragmatic,
programmatic patter of the propaganda of the times
    I woke alone
and white dawn spaces
    colours shake:
the sleeping beauty, either sex, awakes.

The schoolboy smuggled *prostitute* into his private stanza;
    fetched her through a window in his *Pocket
Oxford Dictionary,* all the better to *seduce,*
    and flipping pages, there he stumbles on,
more dimly troubled, *masturbate*
    defined as self-abuse. There's no excuse.
It's sad to think that Latin is no use, and that
Euclidean Geometry lacks colour.
    Ducks is led by Drake. We must reduce The Duke
to an abstract soul in legend
    and there let it self-educe.
Sometimes the cloud-cover makes things outside look duller.
Light as grace comes free with language, good
    as milk and orange juice.

I return to study my own prince of self-importance.
    Give a carrot for his nose. Not grace
but grease is kneaded
    on your knees, with an enormity
in the performance.

Then drops again, with working men
          out dredging something dreadful
from the dregs of port, all wet
and with a foretaste salt. As sure
the sun will set.

Try his invention out in court.
Set him up in a cart. Did thou suppose
thy bliss were royal? Was it not
some squirmy word thou wist to kiss?
          Our princes should not float in boats
of nebular erosis, nor be seen engaging in
          obstreperous ballooning. Favourites hissing
prick his detumescence, leave him
          squittering on the throne.
The old sun god were better dead
before they tip a can of eulogy upon the head
of such a bleeding stone.

He was born, skip all that, in the adolescence,
peeped between adventures in the verbally salacious
and a sense of stranger oddness mirrored
          in blue rooms with silence,
where he took to jazz, imagining as like spontaneous
the sprouting hairs to fuzz, and fantasising
scaling up to blow a scarlet crow,
          with an ideal busk bass replaying ruby blues,
all wails with gurgling quill.

And all the while I had been held between
the thrill and thrall, the trill of tall with frills
and bustling, brushing quivers, feathering
the flight of syllables, the falling smalls,
the brass pretension of the double-quibbles,
born to raise an ideal body of the rivers
from the mouth up to the highest of elated dribbles,
and be bound in essence to be found in deliquescence
      taking pleasures as the prince of givers.
I had been idly fingering my composition.
You could cut Prince Phoebus altogether. Set
the fancy in a hayloft.

      Set the lads and lasses off a-doffing smocks,
except the air is dirty with dry fodder dust,
or write outside, there's such a heat
the moorland sponges sweat
with sticky airs of sleaze, and other must.
Another stream falls to the knees before
the niceties of gender. Farming values
female mammals highly. Goose or gander.
It is politic to give thy music
      some such common sense-agenda.
Writing chicks raise their erotic frocks,
but do not fret. The beauty lusts
      with knees to knock.

Souls at the issue have to choose one or the other.
      Birds show how the tissue flies.
I could be blessed, if thighs enspur
      (if that's a word) the wooded cleft.

The sun rose pink blue orange rose and marigold.
It's long since, like a pair of brothel-creepers,
　　　I'd been climbing up the stairs into the past:
I'm not the one to scale the mast
　　　but to the shingle sing, still sing,
sound still, sound still,
　　　as proud as angels with these curls,
and all the glory of the waters, either
tumbling down the fell or rising
　　　by osmosis up the wall.

His singing-practice in a literal sense
has proved, time out of mind, without exception,
anti-social, and has been described in terms of
squeaking screeches, wailing groans, and sometimes
leaking pipes, and his cracked mind
out of his time spills albumen, and when he moans
　　　you hear how clouds
have covered all the woods of England.

I wish the words might seep as sweet as golden syrup,
　　　not that dark sour silage treacle,
and I might be bobbing in the sally woods,
full of my needs and feeling worth a silver shilling,
　　　I'd have smiling hyssop bedded with sweet marjoram,
and hold the native close to foreign,
　　　going folkish, for to bob a florin
soon, before it's too late.

It is far too late, and the sun has declined
over dingles of dark green. What could be pitied
down the pit is now a picture,
      the senescent wreck,
the old man fancifully flirty
      lost his sex.

And neither is my horticulture any better.
Abstract poetry lets bulbs to sprout at will
and so they leaf in tissue,
      sometimes taking flaccid hops
and getting fizz up tops
between the puddles of emotional paralysis.
It takes a skip to bin what has been theory.
I took a short drive through some forested analysis
      before I let the soul as soil
be wasted to the landfill
      full of unsuccess.

Ye Proud or humble, Wake! The time of Art
is Now! Then how art thou? Some rudeness
is quite nicely scented, driven, derivated
mental as in jouissance to penetrate
the gated walls,
      to perpetrate and plant the world in seed,
variegated, but at best
perpetuate throughout eternity
      a blue grace of the sense of soul.
Forget-me-not. Go back to sleep.
      What sayest thou?

I am still drifting cloud. Let lovers do
all they're allowed. What is the glister
of priapic happiness to me, I mumble.
        I'm not proud I skipped the nappies,
playing cuckoos, hawks and magpies,
trapping flies like swallows, flapping tries
or zapping enemies,
        but win no prize.

Once the sun as a spectacle rose like a lance
        or a lens, with a glance from the glans
to the glens where piping sounds abound:
        the pre-puce colour sticks,
        and slicks to tumbling burns;
an idle tide fills up salt-water gulches
and a mucous gown is cast across the water-courses.

By shrinking gum with providence
        I found a windy harbour this
for impotence. The deadness has me screaming loud,
impatient for the streaming lace

of ruddy cheek and exhalations of the face
        all crumbled in a trembling heap of woodness.

Some dream offices may key in fiction.
We can clear a space to cultivate
        a spiritual art
of hanging knots, of dead
but not forgotten drunks,
of rotted trunks whose creepy-crawlies feed the birds,
also the worms, as meet to eat,
        and depredate predated words.

It seems that in this dream I have acquired a choir
or chorus. Had I not required a chair to see and hear
a show of flesh and air,
        when any lichened rock or root with moss
however wet or dry would do? But this becomes my seat

to sit and see the setting of a pageant of religious grace
and hear the shining brasses hovering
        in blue sun's golden hair, and even higher.

The shades were sort of curtains drawn
with rings, and fall to tumbling; these are either
angels crumbling down the fell-side face
or some comedians with pipes and flutes.

        I look down and there's a tarn
beneath my feet, and it looks deep:
        the iris colours of the lake:
and I thought for a moment of eternal sleep.

Ill dreams

They bore The Corpse of Phoebus

They blew it out in the marsh

They took the way the marches wind

     A salvation army of the mind:

banners of gilt magenta

     reading *Blood & Fire*

the livid sign, the sonance harsh

For this I used a tuning of my own invention.

With their blunt brass instruments they bore

the senex rex for quite a way

into a stillness that was never there before.

FIRST FOREST TARN EPIPHANY

The surface ghost in person disappears
as elf-shine off a forest tarn in conifer;
the mountain lakelet brilliance fades from firs
and water. Fire of bright mentality,
the silver sense of lucence, dance enticement
      tarnishes and vanishes. An airy glitter
of sensation, momentary beauty implantation,
rises and expires evaporation to the skies, just as
Eternity perpetually dies in pine.

A slender flame of fire that flowered up the spine
retires. A light-blaze of the furze subsides.
A peaceful grace of haze, a drift of breeze
across the fellside trees ensues.
A few epiphanies, as proved in time, are prized.

Surface evaporates. The rain relents.
The sun returns to shaft the rising steam.
Reflective coils unwind between the pines.
The spell is bound to shine and calm.
The spectre of a witness drops its qualms.
It is a charm of stillness, mist and light,
a mirrored wetness, image of a present absence
lasts for life. I fancy it recalled intensely
      at my last demise.

THE SYLVAN NOUMENON

I

So to surrender, squander an expenditure of syllables
as standing ghoul before a sylvan noumenon
upon the cusp of its concupiscence
         in glistening, repeated deliquescence,
a salacious squash into a subsidence
         all willowy, sublime
to moan in tone, sporadically blown
up through the fluffed impostures
of imaginary phosphorus, exquisite
         sublimates of stuff...

Along their beds the ripples flood into the floss.
The sun peaks orange and the whole earth groans.
The best of us rejoices, claiming gold for endless loss:
the death of all our voices, nouns and tones.
The world turned strange, went deaf, was dying
         to be buried in the valley of the bones.

So oft is soft, so often off and on
and up and over, besom
         clover, bush and brush.

Well bob me one for ten pence, temperance,
a silver florin:
and remember Rubber Booby All The Day,
The Human Tool before A Sylvan Noumenon:

O Phoebus Rubber Booby, and the sun rose blue
through spectacles of aureate and glass erosis:
      roseate in fact,
the bruise's blush, a rich robust existence in exuberance:
to bob with rubicundity, carol a ditty,
      and come through intact.

So early on I stumbled on
      the nymph of sibling presence,
sylvan noumenon, in private sense renaissance,
various in glory, polysemous in a dress
and daftly mystical: a spiritual woman
with a power of beauty. She could
      bless me to my face, however
riddled with erosion, rock or stand
of trees against semantic waste.

She's dressed in greenness of the yellow saxifrage.
I see her weeping saturated face.
I've seen her intimate with toadflax
      in a crannied nook, and seen
into her sex, sprung sprouts, balsam dicotyledons
burgeoning the bank-side breast.

These lovely cloughs have often been
my scenes of folly, regularly leafless,
miserably melancholy
      when I've lost my song
and the elated carry-on sounds wrong.

II

The glittering shawl cast over life
      is possibly just simply
hawthorn blossom after rain.

      The wind is deaf perhaps
because it has no ears. I hear it
sleeps within a cave within the cliff.

      The rain falls soundlessly across the roof
maybe because it's (really simply) mist
or cloud. It lends itself the shape around
      the skirts of wood.

We come back from the well (or not)
as ghosts of our apparent selves. All humbled.

Lapwings are collapsing.
Hills are riddled with emotional erosion.
Numbers crumbled.

Me, I merely mumbled.

THE LOVE OF ENGLISH

Haslam's Folly

Much must the english love the mulch and slush
that issues from the mouth of miry rough,
the stench of silage from the mix of herbage
     verbiage and roughage, sour queach
given off the rushy moss, mephitis of
a ferrous sump with quaking crust
and all that trickles into tracklessness down valley bottom.

Carr bog issues dissipated from the sodden bent.
We feel our sexes in such soft sog, soppy, soapy stuff
as acid slime, and love
     to shake out filth down in the lovely clough.

Pastured in tufts, or huddled down in pock-hole delf,
the beast is lunching on disconsolation
     in a shadowed patch of field, and puzzles:
Greaves, would they be grooves, as graves, or groves
with leaves of trees, or even kneepads? *Eaves,* not under
roofs or rooves, but down in valley lees? The answer
in the breeze comes as a heave of grief. The vagrant
     breezes rove.

I have been pleased to find real mud in muddles
and a snug of gnosis where I'll nuzzle naze or neb
     in sugars with the bees in clover as in ramson
flowers, leaves and garlic cloves. I've seen real love
     in pairs of common doves.

I slipped onto my knees on being told there really is
no landscape-language linkage: all the rides in pine
are over-run with quibbles, brambles, puns and rhyme.
The pit of farmyard scrap is not the hellhole of the soul.
What pipes and clogs are can't be both
        a drainage problem and a country dance.
The tongue of land between the streams is stricken with disease.
They told me 'arbitrary' isn't choice but chance.

The dogs draw out the intestinal gripes as lights and tripe.
A midden aura draws the flies. My tropes are lies;
I'd fail lingual geology. The horsetail lifts, the stallion stales
        and puddles my apology.

Burns light in sun on glaciated height;
        gills gape and becks entice;
tongue confluence excites;
the spring's conjugal gurgles at the waters' greetings
        quite surpass delight.

A spirit froth like fritters on the hob, a gob of spit,
the wrath of brooks in spate, the bracken breaks
with sudden brakes, and all my woodness is
        consumed in hate. A thing of fate
squats on the sike-side gate.

We suffer loss of moorland twite.
Lapwing, lark, cuckoo and curlew
        also all deplete.

Catastrophe is microwaved
     and laid upon our plate.

Those matin larks that fail were wont to trill
far airier than literary, fairly real and hairy-fairy,
feathered to the bill: *Alauda arvensis,* cry the books
in their Linnaean Latin, singing spokes and epics,
conscious deliquescence, thrilling us while we were
snuggled lovers in a hole down in the heather,
and we heard one singing like a shilling in the sky,
or then another, spilling through the strings of mist
like lace, to grace the shelter we were sat in, or
another early morning when in splendid weather
     the sun peaks orange and the whole earth
speaks its screeches from the rocky face
across a range, the pink cloud-curdling frills,
and there it stays and sings as lodged
     in heights of space.

Cattle graze the field of stars.
The lanes of dales are filled with parked cars.
The spirit flits like bats about all times of year
or day or night. For bats themselves
     the summer dusk is best. Round here
the sun sets in the West.

And neither Nature nor The Loves of English
knows of Progress. Regress yes. Rills gurgle thrills
down in the alder-willow gully. Boys and girls

in musk of summer dusk: a pair take steps
by treads and risers to the disused
railway station down the steeps.
There is a broken room left open. Dawn
wakes to their shouts. Bliss passes out.

Who was it drew the physic from the plot of stars
into my ears, or laced and laded greenwood white
with native cherry-blossom, eh? Who had me
pummelled on the shoulders by the waterfall?
          Whom would you say?

While green wood yet was brown and fields were buff,
the flower trumpets climb the hills with yellow glow
          and call themselves the daffodils.

Some days it is I want to cry, why who am I?
Such depth of pathos surely cannot all be mine.
It could be you down drinking by the stream
white wine in rain. It could be anyone
had bedded down to fire-ash and goodbye this time.

The sun himself looks detumescent through the morning mist.
There must be millions of us have kissed.
And on the bright side of the forest lane, sun shines
again on wetness like a florist bliss:
          marsh-marigold, herb robert, pink purslane.

Into the pit again I'll sink in where I fail.
At Whitsuntide, the Christians say,
       the Holy Ghost came
in between a whistle and a wail.
       The dairy cans were clanging churns;
the churches ringing bells for Anglicans
from hills and out across the plains of England –
Pagans also prancing, boys and girls
       in slips and singlets.

Vernal warbles, audible as little fiddles
on the skirts of waste sound cordial
as curlew curdle: frilly quibbles, risen volume
from the alders and the willows. Also others
really larking strings of lace in space.

Against this place:
long winters largely unrelieved,
the cloughs of leafless trees,
brief lulls under the lees.
       A duller drizzle lingers in another lull
and drops off moss and noses.
Gully trickles down the abject face,
a quiet blubbering as spirits drown,
misled into a mist and close to zero:
       and an exaggerated hopelessness, a place
to dramatise the loss, to curse and magnify
the sad distress, to show the figure
of the self bereft: grief under eaves, and worse,

unhappy groves with nothing left
but stand in mist and freeze.

Brief blips of optimism can be nice; it brightens.
All is fine and dry.
There is another barn of shade
way down on poppy lane.
Well I could keep a few of those,

but sexual sadnesses, it seems to me, strike deeper.

It's not as if
        I could love no-one less but laugh
at me and lasses, in the flesh,
        mistresses,
pull us off by raft across the moss, bring us
silverly titwillow gullible
to glycerine the pillow soft
with careless deliquescence;
ripple into floss and trickle
into tracklessness down valley bottoms.

The draft of image places, less
symbolical than rotten. Fungal.
Something bungled from disguise
into disgrace and other small
disasters and distresses.

This first essay into the Loves of English starts to falter.
I shall try to find a resting-place, a close. OK.
And maybe try again tomorrow.

A score of tricky peewits twisting in the dusk.
The dark end of a row in shadow.
Late-evening back-street engineering works –
Screeches in failing light.

The clank of doings from the bank-side works.
Dank hanging woods down to the brook.
Dark clumps of standing holly,
        wasted dumps, and cloying damps,
the emblems of my sorrow.

The life that clamps the ivy suckers
        up sycamore trunks,
the loud regrets of drunks,
and all these features that may fuck us off
        are mostly just the visage of the ghost of post-
Industrial Melancholy,

Haunting Haslam's Folly.

FINDS PLEASURE IN THE MELANCHOLY

More of the same. The slough debouches,
        waterish, deboshed. Rill trickles
tickling hairgrass round an orifice, and strays
like clerks from offices into a water-hole.

            It lights out of its slit;
It slips its lips: the moss's issue,
labially dribbling puns and quibbles,
riddled like the swallow holes
        with hillside syllables
and squirts of scribble.

            It slips its lips. It tipples
itself sick in a discarded sink. It
        fluffs ephemeral its loves and laughs
to smell its evanescence as a flagrant stink.
It chuffs its obsolescence like a puffer-train
and laughs again at matin larks
        until its songs are all depleted,
and it completely slips its lips. It funks
        and everything gets stuck
and then it prints its sprints,
it lodges logs, ecologies and eclogues
        like the boggart in its clogs.

I read it in a mirror where it sees my face
reflect erosion, all the surface of the earth,
the soil and waste, the scars

of raw exploit. I see it dim hypnogagy
in cinematic scenes of sleep.
I feel its bleating like a sheep.

A one-bar fire in the parlour
and a light left on
for no-one in the hall. The unreal
melancholia of recall.
Look back on all that bacchanal,
the tipples and the falls,
the gurgling well, the fleeting shawl,
the willow and the alder-gullies swirling
flood-spate, eating out
the bank-side wall.

That's an imaginary parlour, an imaginary hall.
A low sharp sun was burning frosted apparitions
off the forest lawn. Hear an
imaginary horn. An unreal form
is seen to flit between the birches
in the morning, looking lost, forlorn. It could be
what they call a faun, or fawn.

And a goose just walked over my grave.
That may not be proved true, for
either it's too soon, or, later on
it's highly likely I'll have been cremated
and my ashes scattered, sentimentally, a little
lacking ceremony, but politely.

But what's that face there in the dark of yew?
A rat? It has the head and tail of privy spirit.

There are ghosts of people drinking to this day
in ghosts of moorland public houses
        raising toasts to vanished brewers,
lovers, causes: here's
to you and yours. The ale carouses time away.

Deep in the snug, I find I'm being questioned by
a Supernatural Goat. The blank spots in the eyes
admit, pass, and perform replies. Goat in a Coat is
the ghost on the coast: the captain
        of the boat of lies. I'm in Eternity inside
its in-turned eyes, and there I float.

I woke on Eden-side. Sandpipers skrike
their wild riparian delights.
        A dream-companion by my side. We took
our breakfast in tents.

Had we not seen the ghost? Not certainly.
A figure in between the lines just disappeared.
It left no tracks of melt, no trace of steps
across the forest lawn, no prints
of bleeding feet, no sign of passage
from the parlour, through the hall, and out
by the main door. And I had no
companion any more. And I heard nothing but

the trickle of some gully water
incising the forest floor. It's clear
I was the one remainder, and this dear void
between the ears is just a space that disappears
like dinosaurs: and there it is
     still flapping its original apparel,
gabbling like a Goose in thick hill fog:
     The Bad God of The Bog.

Whistling blues down shady lane
while lovely night comes out in leaf
and streetlights through the trees
burst into bloom,
it makes me glad to see the moon
leap barefoot from the earth to lace
the rivulets with silver, and the slates
so lately glazed with rain
     share in the shine.

And here I'm heading home to shower
     and to sleep between unusually
freshly-laundered sheets, hoping to meet
     fresh living streams of dreaming
surface-water scenes of starlit physics,
spiritual election, light reflection
     from the puddles that I pass by
chance and choice, to find a cure
and bring a clearness to my lungs and lines
and eyes and ears and dance and voice,

and find a licence to the silence
      sluiced in water-lucence,
hoping to re-fantasize my forking soul
is ringing like a pair of tuning tines:
      it's like a spiritual greed.
I hope to let you know if I succeed.

The glittering shawl cast over life is possibly
just simply hawthorn-blossom after rain
caught in the sun.
      The wind is deaf perhaps because it has
no ears. I hear it sleeps
down in a cave beneath the cliff that's been
its domicile for years.

The rain falls soundlessly across the roof,
happen because it's only mist or cloud,
the same as shapes around the skirts of wood.
I'd show you proof of all I claim here if I could.
I'd try to over-ride the jeers of all my peers.
      The deaf wind cries aloud.

We come back from the well, like home from school,
ghouls of ourselves, some more aloof and proud,
but others humbled, each with tales to tell
of terrible encounters with our fears:

The Lapwings Are Collapsing!
All the hills are riddled with emotional erosion!
Numbers crumbled!
Me, I failed!
    I had this speech to make
but merely mumbled
    and broke up in tears.

How pretty petty little birds sing their
hilltop peripety. The glitter clears and here is seen
wan water when bright shaws are sheen
    and lit by light with heat
the singing birds re-spring their repetitions
    neat and clean,

a seepage out of sylvan heaven,
    the dementia repeats, as in, say,
see page seventy-seven.

Sounding Secularly Holy

Quack
I feel a cure for woodness working very slow.
    I really love Nobody though it lifts me
nearly, just to say *I love,* I love the, love the *thee*
however bodiless this singularity appears to be.
    I love the poetry of poor John Clare:
    And Mare blobs stain with gold the meadow drain:
I love the lovely low marsh marigold, it is so
      green and yellow; and I'd like to clear a space
for more frivolity, and O!
    I love to hear a Blackburn blackbird curling
alveolar trills, the shrilling rhyming with the colour
of its bill. And then again, I like as well
    to hear a pentatonic melody made up
of minor thirds; also some jolly Latin terms: the faint
vulgarity of *Turdus, merula* or *philomelos,* and their loves
of snails and worms. It strikes me I quite like the common
world of birds, and have been rather fond of the
    illusions of profundity, and colour-names of words.
The *aube,* englobed in rubicundity;
the ruddy dawn, aura aurora, haloed bluish yellow glaze,
and the fresh yearly greenery; the faintly literary scenery
of phrases such as *post-romantic haze,*
    the mere idea of more arcadian days, and here it is:
the wandering *faunus* of the ways! Hello Good Fellow!
What? And has tha' come to warn us? Running back
from woodness into soreness, and it's odd
but that familiar little god has just slipped back into

its rushy bed. I think it said that
Nobody itself is dead.

Free festive bacteria delight
in the decay abounding
round the mouth and down
the valley of the bones.

There's still a fair amount of pollutant about.

They drove a digger through the withy
scattering the tattered new-age fogeys
who were running wild, emitting shouts
and littering the wood with spillage and abusive nouns.
(New Ages are the French for Clouds;
Some Images are Clones, and some are Clowns,
and some are folkish bogeys. I've become so
yokel-local-focal that quite homely villages
appear Gigantic Towns –
The madness of the age I shared with boggarts
and their brothers brought me down.)

It seems to me, where aspiration fails
it has to de-aspire, and disappear
before the onset of despair; but that was when
it mattered to me badly, being battered in a lay-by
by the wind, with one flat tyre beyond repair
and not another one to spare. I said bye-bye

to my inflation, sadly, then and there.
Somewhere in either Lancashire or Wales.

Seed blows in air. It settles far or near: far on
the salt-sea flats its fails its finish, perishes; or near
here on the fields it settles and may flourish
        and proliferate, mimetic or genetic, undiminished.

For solace: cloth for streaming ruddy cheek:
        a mop of heavy cotton lace
wrung from a bucket: wipe thy face
and try to speak. *Ah, fuck it!*

The sun peaks orange and the whole earth sings
        See how the spring-line glitters!
on this patch. See how we've seen the passing
        of a deep depression, fetched
across the oceanic earth. See how we've seen
how waters run as wild as scribble, yet they keep
their courses, and repeatedly, and audible,
        the bird-life quibbles into titters.

I might have reached the end of this, my *Music*. I'll conclude a
coda with a verse of general notes as proses:
        What's well here is no hole but really merely bank-side
springs and moor-side issues. These are strictly hills as
peneplainal spurs, and some way South of fells. How constant
rivers kept their courses we may know by names. My love of
english covers just a segment of the glory of the Southern North,

for what it's worth: the streaming waters down a dene, a vale, a valley, but assimilated to the dales. Clough, sike and brook can be felt merging Northward into gutter, dike, burn, beck. We hold to water, neither forces though, nor scales, but falls. The grain of sandstone makes it good for walls. The grazing's mainly cattle, sheep and horses.

Life of course is more emotional than water-courses, and the rush can feel sensational as crime, while fetching prizes from a mire of slime. The runnel course is ultimately gravitational as the sad force is.

As for the self it's my misfortune and encumbrance to have had, he'd rather celebrate an utter silliness of sill and gutter, say I'm sure I saw my trunks are shorn all for to coppice my resources, verses, voices and occasional remorses, cries, cares, clauses, courses, causes, cures, metamorphoses.

Meanwhile he'll be up each morning stacking piles of woodness for the winter in the clapped-out caravan, the shed of things he keeps in cold remembrance that he lived and loved, it may be said, and later on would have been dead, and so it closes. I have made most of this up out of my head, among the brambles and the brier-roses.

Appendix: It (1997)

for Robert Sheppard

[It]

posits the creative element
in writing as a faculty of *It,* what it
refers to, and by trick, syntactic sleight, an *It*
that has no antecedent but itself, an entity
made of nonentity, a spirit fancy that itself
can predicate, creating comprehensible the world itself,
envisaged as projected *It.* As I imagine it
projected it fends for, it defends, itself. It may as well
take flower form and sprout and seed itself itself.

As I imagine it imagines and responds, free spirit
creativity, investing each imagined image with itself.

So as I posit it is posited it posits itself positive,
a something out of nothing that can find and read
the traces of itself across the writing of another, anyone
who's had it activated in her, in his, plan.

And so it reads itself adventures in poetic history,
how it made an immanent poetics. It explains itself
the principle and principal that multiplies itself
in figments of dramatic form.

If it imagines Nature, even Cosmic Nature, even that
is not so much its antecedent as the living faculty it has
to theorize and speculate itself about.

But it's a trick, a sleight, a something now you see it and
a nothing now you don't. It's like a sly evasive wit, I said,
in an oblique allusion to a pure illusion without substance,

immaterial. A quondam nothing that may yet accept
constraints of reason, sonnet form, take logic or
syntactic language or the discipline of mathematics
if it chooses what's conducive to it. It may not.
Since its conception is entirely in whatever the imagination is,
it is irrational, and may be that which must be inadmissible
in any rational, materialist, non-metaphysical
theoretical poetics. Maybe such must do without it, but
it isn't bound to give assent to anything
that may be made with it left out.
It's irreducible as nothing else is. It's invocable
in vocatives of O *Creative Spirit, come and help me*
to describe it in poetics. I have made provision for it
in a partial thesis of it, as a lure for its approval:
that such features of a modern writing practice
as are commonly referred to self-reflexive self-reflection,
or to para-language, meta-language, or the writer's sexuality,
are side effects and by-products of it-projection, it
in its projection from whatever self.

As it takes over self's imagination, imaging its situation
in whatever really is,
      as it takes over me it will include me and my language
in what shapes its world
      the poem takes, however close to fact or multiplied
in speculative fiction,
      taking over the imagination it includes the writer,
sex and language in the shape of scope it takes.

It makes itself in presence conscious;
it unmakes itself, unconscious in its absence. Present / absent
playing chess, doing arithmetic, or playing with the prepositions
in internal space of kinaesthetics in cognition, it appears
and disappears into the space of that which it creates.
It generates the diagrams of that which might describe it
in relation to the world. Sometimes you have to shut it up
inside some sort of box to get less mindful labours done.

But when you write with it, it's in the pen. Its point
is a projection of the wriggle of the fingers and a subtle
writhing of the wrist. It moves along by ballpoint, rollerball
or nib from left to right and back again. I stop. It stops,
as if to point its nose in air, and sniff, and think.

It scratches, echoes of inscription, scribbles of descriptive sketches,
quill and inkpot through to tapping fingertips of type,
selecting apposites from cluster, grip, grope, gripe or grasp
whatever grape is ripe. It chooses choices as to texture, sense
and voice. It gambles, rambles in perambulation, gambols
careless if it illustrates a common wealth of mind or not. Can it
go straight? Could I not write without it? Where's the point?

Since it was generated as a something out of nothing
by syntactic sleight, is it linguistic category-mistake?
It doesn't think so, since, released from language, it can
recognise itself out on the street, in bright animal wit,
or in the moving point of melody in music. It can plot
its own de-cadence, even as you sense it fail, err,
hesitate in loss, in line.

You pick it up again in lines and lives of others, how it seems
to sew a thread between the writer and the reader. It's a
needle-point that leaves its scratches on the record where it jumps.

It's there to be enjoyed, the way it draws the writer and the language
in its scope, how it enjoys its prior subject self
as that from which it must derive.

So it describes me in its own descriptions, just as it inscribes
the form it takes, the way it makes its essays in poetics,
how it issues in what's taken for my speech,
how it is faceted with forms of reference,
how it flares out of frame in a presence of mind, how it's
in fluency, in some intensity, until its seizures cease.

Then when it's gone you can dissect it in its absence
and it isn't, as if wasn't, as if it were never there. Each of its little deaths
is repetition. Now unlocked from language it has gone from
the enclosure of a tongue. You see it play on body borders
manifest in genius at sport, or spring alert in action
in emergency. And now again it comes alive in language,
accurately phonic in particularity to qualities of psychic aura,
be they clear or crackle, risen hackle, soft as fluff is cushion,
or a spike with hob and tang, a clout with head and tail, or as
a fork the way it tines. Or when it went again more syrupy
and doleful in its dirges for the body that it's left in disbelief
again gone dead.

As soon as I project it, I can see that it's not me; it's that not-me
that predicates more than I can. It could be Genius,
and that's not me. It gets inflated in a Cult of Spirit.
That's not me. It can ignite the stars of popular celebrity.
It's there in any charismatic feat of skill.

I said it's like saliva. Maybe it's like ichor in charisma.
It incites a fear like a taboo. It finds itself excluded
from the offices of ordinary prose. Whole swathes
of working life will not admit it. It escapes to twitter
over dreams asleep. It's seen to flare, flame, flaunt itself
in violent excitements on the streets at night.
It's like an imp of mischief caught and blinded
in the headlights of police. We can deny it and forget it,
say it's not important, let its skin go limp,
        its something flit.

It doesn't end. As I imagine it again, I see it has a history.
As I remember it I read it back to basics in the classics,
pagan spirit intellect in fact. It's in Renaissance forms
of English Language figuration, operating under a Platonic Licence;
it's in mint proliferation, at the root; in Personification.

It gets blamed, attainted for enthusiasm that it inspires.
It's taken strange and bloody forms of madness in Religion.
In the dull sunlight and gravity of Reason, under taint
of superstition it occults itself and hides in such retreats
as classical translation, and in animus of personal wit and spite.
Or lies, relaxed, elastic, in pentameters of pastoral iambic.

Come again, Romantic in Inflation, it's Divine Imagination.
Then it animates World Dialectics, ingenuities of Capital
and Messianic Hopes that swell the populace as well.
It nearly dies, drowned, stifled in the filth of waters
and the filth of smoke. It comes into the shambles
and it gets cut down. It lives its leaves, it leaves
its parts dismembered, everywhere around.

I imagine it has rights in propositions made about it.
It abides as close to senses as the eye selects its sights;
in ear it foregrounds certain sounds; or in inflections
of the tongue, in the configurations it describes
with prepositions in constructed as invented space.
O Human Spirit! You can see it in intoxication
on the dregs of its estate, and feel its phobia,
its fear and flight from forms of stiflement.

I'd celebrate it simply but I can't forget: it is a scandal:
        how it sucks to patronage in any age:
how it might at any moment prostitute itself for forms of payment
drawn on forces of corrective right, and how it's rightly been to blame
for cruel mayhem. Abject it may die of shame, then may it
pray to some transcendent Bod or Gob to be made good.
        It may go straight
to seek employment in the service of whatever idol ideology
may offer it exertive space. It may rise and shine in the fat-face
feline wit of privileged executive. It takes all blame and shame
into its sham of nothing and comes on again with glitterings
of lips and fingers, coursing on the blood.

The now that's news of its originality is nearly drowned
in what's around. Critique made in its absence may have
had it fixed as victim in a rifle-sight. It triggers that.

Its oscillation, absence / presence, life and death or sleep and wake,
produces shape in history as plot. Its aftermath or after-life is
death-in-life, dull absence where it's not. It comes to life in
folklore-like revival, in the myths of its survival everywhere, in
all things great and small. It is ironical in self-denial. It is
curiously identical with anything
          that's individual on any scale.

I have it posited as positive with head and tail, a history
by way of trail, a litter, tracery of glitter written in its
literary light, and that dull fail in dumps of infill.
If you can see what I mean, we could talk about it: how
its presence in alertness is accommodated in ecologies
in evolution; how its antique spiritual vocabulary might be
if not retained, retrained on trellises of the imaginary
secular noun; how the sense of it has therapeutic use; how
a poetics might be built in its light; and what to do with how it
imbricates in rhythm, rhyme, and tricks of sound;
          how it adapts to prose.

How it braces as it faces and it passes tests in sex and classes
its technique through pure theoretical critique, of text. Its death and its
revival. Its survival. What it meets with now and next may be a
Darwinist totality unchecked: a Nature-Flood that sweeps away
not only antique spirit, soul in myth, but also fences and defences
          that made cultural and social space.

That last may be no threat,
        that it may float.

A hard head-heart of undeceived and disenchanted shadow,
quite demystified and itless as a frame of mind
is only one bet one might lay and try to live by
to survive.

My bet is that the charm and the enchantment of it
warm more than the antique cockles of a heart.

As it evolves it may be what
survives itself as love and lust for life.
It may just possibly be accurate to call it spirit

By a lubrick of ovum and sperm
By spittle
By a technical sleight or a slippery trick
        in its continuing creation it's
worth living for; it's loveable, however little.
        And that's it.

BIOGRAPHICAL NOTE

MICHAEL HASLAM was born in Bolton, Lancashire in 1947, and educated at Bolton School and Peterhouse, Cambridge. Initially published in the network associated with 'The Cambridge School of Poetry' in the 1960s and early '70s, he became widely known through the publication, to great acclaim, of his collected poems, *A Whole Bauble* (Carcanet, 1995). A revised and reconsidered edition of this work has recently been published under the title *Mid Life* by Shearsman Books in 2007.

In 1970 he moved to Foster Clough, near Hebden Bridge in the Calder Valley and, as he says "by the late 1970s merely living here had become my sole poetic subject". He still lives in the same house.

Having worked as a labourer most of his life, thanks to a legacy he is now able to devote his time to writing.

Recent titles in Arc Publications'
POETRY FROM THE UK / IRELAND,
include:

SHANTA ACHARYA
Dreams that Spell the Light

LIZ ALMOND
The Shut Drawer
Yelp!

JONATHAN ASSER
Outside The All Stars

JAMES BYRNE
Blood / Sugar

DONALD ATKINSON
In Waterlight: Poems New, Selected & Revised

JOANNA BOULTER
Twenty Four Preludes & Fugues on
Dmitri Shostakovich

THOMAS A CLARK
The Path to the Sea

TONY CURTIS
What Darkness Covers
The Well in the Rain

JULIA DARLING
Sudden Collapses in Public Places
Apology for Absence

CHRIS EMERY
Radio Nostalgia

KATHERINE GALLAGHER
Circus-Apprentice
Carnival Edge: Selected Poems

CHRISSIE GITTINS
Armature

MICHAEL HASLAM
The Music Laid Her Songs in Language
A Sinner Saved by Grace

MICHAEL HULSE
The Secret History

BRIAN JOHNSTONE
The Book of Belongings

JOEL LANE
Trouble in the Heartland

TARIQ LATIF
Punjabi Weddings

HERBERT LOMAS
The Vale of Todmorden
A Casual Knack of Living: Collected Poems

PETE MORGAN
August Light

MARY O'DONNELL
The Ark Builders

MICHAEL O'NEIL
Wheel

IAN POPLE
An Occasional Lean-to

PAUL STUBBS
The Icon-Maker

SUBHADASSI
peeled

LORNA THORPE
A Ghost in My House

MICHELENE WANDOR
Musica Transalpina
Music of the Prophets

JACKIE WILLS
Commandments
Fever Tree